there is no ~~oven~~ _pork_
in
inang's kitchen

Magida Najjar and Francis Perez

ISBN 978-621-95767-0-3

Perez Publishing
Cainta, Rizal, Philippines
First Printing 2019

Photography:
Francis Perez
Magida Najjar
Hashim M. Najjar
Thess Ramirez-Montuya
Maureen Montuya
Arthur Montuya
Dhan Michael Yabut
Marideth Macaso-Perez

Text:
Francis Perez
Magida Najjar
Marideth Macaso-Perez

For mummuye and puppuye,

and the many hearts they had touched

about the authors

Francisco Perez or Okiks to relatives and friends, and Francis in business setting, is self-employed. He is the president of an IT corporation he established with a set of good, long-time friends.

Okiks has three children – Noah, Nani and Ana – and a grandchild, Tantan. All of them are now his best buddies.

Magida Najjar is a self-declared good cook and a food lover. She maintains the foodie website "www.mymotherskitchens.com." She is a human resources and communications professional, a quilter, crafter, and was a hospital volunteer. She lives in Saudi Arabia with her husband, Hashim; she is a happy wife and a mother of three Saudi boys – Danyal (God bless his soul), Adnan and Yousif.

Magida Najjar is also Ellen Perez, as she was commonly known before her marriage to Hashim. Magida is the name she adopted when she converted to Islam, which is, by the way, NOT the reason there is no pork in her mother's (Inang) kitchen.

Francis and Magida are siblings, along with three others. After them are Perry (God bless his soul), Zarah and Jakc. Francis is one year older than Magida and the rest were distanced by two years each, making Francis and Magida responsible for their siblings after their parents as is the case in many Filipino households. As a result, they became partners (in crime), while developing into dependable adults. They were, however, separated when Magida went to Saudi Arabia as an overseas contract worker, got married and settled in her husband's country. Despite the distance, Francis and Magida remain close through love, trust, inter-dependence which are all watered by deep friendship and constant communication. Some of their emails and phone calls are about recipes, Inang's recipes mostly -- the main reason for the birth of this book.

acknowledgement

Many thanks to Inang (now in heaven) for her desire to have her recipes collected; because of that, this book was conceived. While the book unfolds, the support of some of the people we know flows. The following are worth mentioning – in no particular order:

Sam Oomen, for his consistent push to get the recipes collected. His tips on formatting, photography, etc. Sam drops by my office every now and then, and inspires me with his gentle follow up. If he does not find me, he leaves a small note to say that he was around. Sam, thank you.

Edenella Nia Colinayo for the graphic design. Nia is the cousin of Rochelle Jaye Granali, who is an interior designer and friend of the family. Nia and I coordinated electronically for this book because of distance: Philippines and Saudi Arabia. The first time we met in person was when she showed me her finished part of the work. She taught me how to use InDesign and I ended up subscribing for the application - with pleasure. Thank you, Nia. We should work together again.

Dhan Michael Yabut for the photo-shooting tips and for kitchen testing one of the recipes. We know he would have done more testing, had we asked. I have no doubt. Dhan, thanks.

To this wonderful family: Thess Ramirez-Montuya, Arthur Montuya and Maureen Ramirez-Montuya for their huge contribution to this project. They have done most of the kitchen-testing the recipes. I admire their attention to details and patience in re-testing recipes to capture the taste, and sometimes the look, of Inang's cooking. Thess and I were constantly chatting or on the phone as she asks for clarification and to critic the recipe's instructions. "Where is the salt in the instructions?" she would exclaim. "Saltless, the recipe is saltless," my excuse. That would be enough to start a series of jokes and laughter. Thess and I were best friends in high school and she knows well that mom's cooking could be salty. Arthur helped in photography and Maureen was the boss in the photo-exchange. That's a team!

My other siblings and their spouses - Zarah and Mike Moreno, Jake and Marideth Perez - for their recipe contributions and many vital tips.

Magida's kids -- Danyal (God bless his soul), Adnan and Yousif for their love and for sampling the dishes with gusto. I have made Filipinos of them although they were born and have been living in Saudi Arabia. :-)

Tantan, Francis' grandson, for his positive wit and as a source of inspiration to his lolo (grandfather).

Hashim Najjar, for taking on most of Magida's responsibilities at home so she can concentrate on cooking and writing part of this book. Hashim's willingness and patience in wandering the Saudi local market and frequenting the supermarkets of Khobar, Dammam and Qatif for Filipino food ingredients was awesome. Hashim is also our editor. I always keep in mind "when in doubt, reach out," and Hashim would be there. "Shukran, Sayed."

To all our friends (Francis' and mine) who had genuine interest in the completion of this book. We are thankful for your support.

introduction

"Inang" is a traditional Filipino term that means "mother." However these days, Inang is used to refer to an older woman as a term of respect. In this book, Inang is our biological mom because that was how we called her when we were younger. Sometime later in our grown-up years, our sister, Zarah, insisted that Inang is too traditional and "baduy" (uncool) that we should shift to calling our mother "mommy." We found her suggestion hilarious, but as she continued calling Inang mommy, we followed suit. So, now we know who is more dominant among Inang, err, mommy's siblings!

"There is no oven in Inang's kitchen" is a true statement. There never was, so all the recipes in this book do not require an oven. We mean "no baking." Just genuinely basic and traditional Filipino food from oldies to popular – but from the kitchen and hands of our Inang.

"There is no pork in Inang's kitchen" is another true statement. In my dad's family, we do not cook nor do we eat pork, hence this book can also be called "no-pork cookbook." Inang and Amang (our dad) do not eat pork and they raised us similarly.

Now, it was usual for Inang to ask one of us, her kids, to get a pen and a sheet of paper. Depending on the time of day, she would either dictate a letter for a long-distance relative or a grocery list. She had this strange insecurity that her handwriting was not legible enough. So, to tease her, we would make fun of her chicken-scratch scripts, but still go on taking dictation from her. The exercise afforded us bonding moments with her. If the dictation were for a grocery list, the list-taker would be her companion in the palengke (market). As children, we knew we could ask her to buy us something else, and she rarely said no! Later on, as adults, we loved her appeal that we pay for her groceries and other items. We called her "bilmoko*," but her requests always made us feel special.

---

* A novelty song by Fred Panopio celebrates the Pinoy bilmoko as a chronic solicitor of anything she fancies. That she wants her man "to buy me this and that" indicates not only her bargaining ability but her sharp economic sense. https://www.sunstar.com/ph/article/377089

Our introduction to life in Inang's kitchen started from those note-taking exercises. Francis being the eldest was earliest to be Inang's kitchen aide. From there, his exposure to life extended outside the kitchen, long before he was eight years of age! Francis became a responsible young man while he was still a boy!

Through the years, we had seen Inang's interest to entertain her friends with her cooking. Budget was her only restraint in earlier days. While it did not completely stop her from that passion, her cooking gave birth to different recipes that are from scratch and some a deviation from the norm, a few of them are in this book.

You will find this book a good introduction to Filipino cooking as it documents the basic way of cooking Pinoy (Filipino) dishes without the use of instant fixes and mixes -- with due respect to the now popular practice -- plus how the same recipes were wonderfully produced by Inang's loving hands. You will also find not-so-common dishes that could introduce new ideas or twists to what you already know. A bigger plus are Inang's cooking tips which we get from merely watching her; she quickly shared those secrets when we asked. She was generous with her recipes and generous with everything. This book will also provide a very small glimpse of the life my Inang lived.

This book is not a collection of Filipino recipes. It is a compilation of a Filipina's home-cooked meals which were enjoyed not only by her husband and children, but by her many relatives, friends, and visitors. If you are a Pinoy, about half of the ingredients in all the recipes would already be in your kitchen, while the rest are easily available in your local market. If you are a non-Pinoy, this would be a worthy primer on Filipino cooking as it will help you make up a simple Filipino kitchen. We aim to take you away from scratching your head while mumbling "which one here?" because you will also find that any recipe from any category is perfect any day.

We hope you find this book for keeps. Our wish is that it becomes one of your favorites. Magida has three favorite cookbooks from a shelf that holds more than a hundred. Our ultimate wish is for this to become one in your three or four -- or even one in your 10 favorite cookbooks!

P.S. We used the original titles in the recipe, so you would find some in Tagalog while the others in English or a combination (Taglish, as we term it). We tried as much as possible to provide its English translation.

table of contents

appetizers, salads and soups

macaroni soup

Prep Time: 25 minutes

Cooking Time: 25 minutes

Serves: 6 to 8

Ingredients:

- 250g ground chicken
- 1 small onion, chopped
- 3 cloves garlic, minced
- 1 medium carrot, julienned
- 100g green beans, thinly sliced
- 1 small red bell pepper, finely diced
- 100g cabbage shredded
- 200g macaroni pasta, boiled until al-dente
- vegetable oil
- salt and pepper to taste
- 1 cup milk (fresh or evap milk)
- 3 tbsp patis
- 4 cups water

Instructions:

1. Sautee garlic in vegetable oil until golden. Add onions and cook until they are transparent. Add ground chicken and cook until half done.

2. Add carrots and green beans.Stir for about two minutes then add red bell pepper and cabbage. Stir again for a few minutes then add water, macaroni, salt, and pepper. Leave to boil then lower the heat.

3. Add milk and patis and simmer for another two minutes.

4. Serve hot.

sotanghon soup

Prep Time: 15 minutes

Cooking Time: 1 hour

Serves: 6 to 10

Ingredients:

- 1kg whole chicken
- 500g sotanghon noodles, soaked in water
- 1 medium onion, quartered
- 1-inch ginger
- 1 bunch young onion, divided
- 100g Chinese cabbage, cut into 2-inch pieces including the whitish part
- salt and pepper to taste
- fish sauce to taste
- 6 cups water
- fried garlic to garnish (optional)

Instructions:

1. Clean chicken and put in a casserole along with water, onion, half the bunch of young onion, ginger, salt and pepper. Let boil.

2. Lower the heat and simmer until the chicken is done. Yes, at this stage, the chicken is still whole!

3. Add patis and adjust according to taste.

4. Remove the chicken from the casserole, let cool and shred by hand or with the use of two forks, discarding the bones. Set the shredded chicken meat aside.

5. Serve soup in separate bowls by portioning noodles, soup water, shredded chicken, young onion leaves and Chinese cabbage.

6. Add a touch of fried garlic, if using. Serve hot.

 # arroz caldo

Prep Time: 15 minutes

Cooking Time: 40 minutes

Serves: 4 to 5

Ingredients:

- 1kg chicken, cut into serving pieces
- 1-1/2 cup glutinous rice (malagkit)
- 6 cloves garlic, minced
- 1 medium onion, diced finely
- 2-inch ginger, peeled and grated
- 6-7 cups water
- 2 hard-boiled eggs, sliced
- salt and pepper to taste
- 1/4 cup fish sauce
- fried garlic and spring onions to garnish

Instructions:

1. Sautee ginger in oil until light brown; add garlic and onions and stir for 2 minutes. Add chicken and stir again until the pinkish juices come out.

2. Add rice. Stir. Add water, let boil and simmer until the rice are cooked through in the consistency that you prefer, adding more water, as necessary. The chicken would be cooked by then. Add salt, pepper and fish sauce.

3. Serve with slices of hard boiled eggs, fried garlic and green onions as garnishing.

One or two cubes of chicken bouillon would help in the chicken taste, if you prefer. In this case, you would adjust the amount of salt/fish sauce.

It is also known as chicken lugaw. I usually requested Inang to cook this for me everytime I come home to the Philippines from Saudi Arabia and it would be ready upon my arrival.

This dish is well-loved by my hubby and kids, more popular during winter time as it provides heat. This is also my hubby's comfort food.
(Magida)

atsarang papaya

Prep Time:
45 minutWes

Cooking Time:
30 minutes

Ingredients:

- 2kgs green papaya, grated
- 3 medium carrots (about 1/4kg), diced finely, a few were cut into florets
- 2 red bell pepper (about 1 cup), diced finely
- 15-18 shallots, sliced thinly in rings
- 1/2kg singkamas (turnips), diced finely
- 1 cup raisins
- 3 tbsps salt
- 1 cup sugar

Pickling solution:
- 1/4kg ginger root, sliced thinly
- 1-1/2 cup white vinegar

Inang has a version of atsarang papaya that includes pineapple tidbits. As this adds sweetness to the taste of the atsara, she reduces the amount of sugar.

Instructions:

1. Sprinkle 3 tbsps of salt onto grated papaya, leave for about 15 minutes to drain, then squeeze by hand to remove its juice.

2. Mix vinegar, sugar and ginger over medium heat and simmer for 3-5 minutes, almost to boiling point. Remove from heat and let cool until warm to the touch. Drain, keep the solution and discard the ginger.

3. Mix the rest of the ingredients separately.

4. Pour ginger-vinegar onto papaya mixture. Transfer to jars.

gisadong bagoong

Prep Time:
10 minutes

Cooking Time:
20 minutes

Ingredients:

- 1 bottle* of bagoong
- 1/2 bottle* of vinegar
- 2 calamansi or 1 medium lemon
- lemon rind strips, if using lemon
- 3 cloves garlic, minced
- 2 tbsp cooking oil
- 4 tbsp sugar (or to taste)

Instructions:

1. Mix bagoong, vinegar, calamansi of lemon (and rind strips) and sugar. Boil them over medium heat until liquid has evaporated. Set aside.

2. Brown garlic in oil over low fire. Mix garlic in bagoong.

3. Add sugar to taste.

Bagoong or "shrimp paste" is available in grocery stores in jars.

In the instructions above, measure the vinegar using the same bottle that contained the bagoong.

gulay at bagoong

Prep Time:
15 minutes

Ingredients:

- gisadong bagoong (recipe on preceeding page)
- steamed okra
- fresh ampalaya (bitter gourd), sliced very thinly
- fresh labanos (raddish), sliced very thinly
- fresh tomato, sliced

Fresh ampalaya and labanos, tomatoes and steamed okra

Steamed fish

Instructions:

Serve the vegetables with bagoong and vinegar to accompany fried/grilled/smoked fish.

Other vegetables that can be used with grilled, fried or smoked fish are steamed kangkong, steamed talbos ng kamote (sweet potato tops), etc.

Fried fresh fish

Steamed fish

Fried dried fish

atsarang talong at ampalaya

Prep Time:
10 minutes

Cooking Time:
10 minutes

Ingredients:

- 1 medium ampalaya (bitter gourd)
- 2 medium eggplants
- 2 pcs serrano chili
- 1-inch piece ginger, sliced
- 1/2 cup quartered or sliced shallots
- 1 tbp black pepper corns
- 1 tsp salt
- 1/4 cup vinegar
- 1/4 cup water
- 1/4 cup sugar

Instructions:

1. Mix all ingredients in a casserole simmer in medium heat until vegetables are half done. Do not stir.

2. Leave to cool and keep in a tight-lid container.

3. Can be stored for a week.

lumpiang shanghai

Prep Time:
1 hour

Cooking Time:
15 minutes

Serves:
4 to 5

Ingredients:

- 1kg ground beef
- 1 cup singkamas (turnips), diced finely
- 1/2 cup carrots, diced finely
- 1/2 cup, onions diced finely
- 1 egg
- 2 tbsps all-purpose flour
- salt and pepper to taste
- lumpia wrapper (spring roll pastry)
- cooking oil for deep-frying
- 1 tbsp all-purpose flour and 4 tbsps water for sealing the edges of lumpia wrapper

Instructions:

1. Mix all ingredients in a bowl.

2. Measure about 1 tbsp of the mixture and wrap in lumpia wrapper, sealing edges with a mixture of flour and water.

3. Deep fry in hot oil until golden brown.

This is Inang's original recipe. Through the years, in my own kitchen, I had changed it by sautéing the ground beef with onions then mixing them with the rest of the ingredients before wrapping in pastry. I omit the egg. This takes less frying time, too.
(Magida)

okoy

Prep Time:
45 minutes

Cooking Time:
45 minutes

Serves:
5 to 6

Ingredients:
- 5 cups sweet potatoes, shredded
- 3 cups pumpkin, shredded
- 1/8 tsp salt
- 1/8 tsp sugar
- shrimps for topping

Batter:
- 1 cup glutinous rice flour
- 1 egg white
- salt and pepper, to taste
- 1 tbsp baking powder
- 1 cup shrimp water (refer to page 92)
- 2 tbsp juice of achuete seeds

Dip:
- 1 cup white vinegar
- 1 tsp sugar
- 1 tbsp freshly ground black pepper
- 1 tsp salt
- minced garlic (optional)

Instructions:

1. Mix sweet potatoes and pumpkin. Sprinkle with about a teaspoon each of salt and sugar and mix again.

2. Put a tablespoon of batter in a small plate followed by the okoy mix. Top with shrimps. Cover with a tablespoon of batter and deep fry over high heat until light brown.

3. Drain in paper towels or on a sieve. Serve while hot.

Leave the shredded sweet potatoes and pumpkins under the sun for about 10 minutes to dry them a bit. This would produce crispier okoy. (Magida)

  # fresh lumpia

Prep Time: 30 minutes

Cooking Time: 15 minutes

Serves: 4 to 5

Ingredients:

- 1/2kg shrimps, shelled, deveined and sliced
- 4 cloves garlic, minced
- 1 big onion, diced finely
- 2 cups singkamas (turnips), julienned
- 1/2 cup green beans, julienned diagonally
- 1 cup carrots, julienned
- 1 cup sweet potatoes, cubed
- salt and pepper to taste
- water
- lettuce leaves
- spring roll pastry

Instructions:

1. Sautee garlic and onion until transparent. Add shrimps and cook while stirring until shrimps are pinkish in color.

2. Add green beans, carrots and sweet potatoes. Stir for half a minute and add half a cup of water. Stir again until half done – about 2 minutes.

3. Add turnips, salt and pepper and stir for another minute. Leave to cool.

4. Top one spring roll pastry with lettuce leaf. Spoon over about half a cup of lumpia mixture and roll to wrap.

5. Top with sauce and garnishing.

> Tapioca starch is a good substitute for cornstarch.

For the sauce:
- 3 tbsps soy sauce
- 1/2 cup sugar
- 3 tbsps cornstarch
- 2-1/2 cups 1ater
- 1/2 tsp ground pepper
- 1 tbsp peanut butter (optional)
- 5 cloves garlic, minced very finely

Instructions:

Mix all ingredients (except garlic) in a casserole and let simmer over medium heat until boiling point. Add garlic.

Garnish:

Mixed ground peanuts and sugar

beef and chicken

beef and
chicken

atay at balun-balunan adobo

 Prep Time: **30 minutes**

 Cooking Time: **40 minutes**

Serves: **3 to 4**

Ingredients:

- 1/2kg chicken liver
- 1/2kg chicken gizzard
- 1 head garlic, minced and divided (half to be used in sauteeing)
- 1/2 cup vinegar
- freshly-ground black pepper
- 2 pcs dried red chilis
- 3 tbsps soy sauce
- dash of sugar
- 4 tbsps cooking oil

Instructions:

1. Clean chicken gizzard well, removing the film-like skin from inside. Make little slits on each piece.

2. Clean chicken liver.

3. Mix liver, gizzard, half of the minced garlic and half the vinegar in a pan and let boil. Do not stir. Drain.

4. Sautee remaining garlic in oil.

5. Add gizzard to the pan and stir for about a minute. (yes , you would have to chose the gizzards and leave the liver for now)

6. Add remaining vinegar and simmer until gizzards are tender (about 10 minutes) adding water if necessary, but conservatively.

7. Add chicken liver and mix well.

8. Add soy sauce, dash of sugar, ground black pepper and chilis. Simmer for 10 more minutes without stirring.

chicken feet adobo

Prep Time: 45 minutes

Cooking Time: 45 minutes

Serves: 4 to 5

Ingredients:

- 1/2kg chicken feet, cleaned and cut into two pieces, crosswise)
- 1 head garlic, minced and divided (half to be used in sauteeing)
- 1/2 cup vinegar
- 1 tsp whole black pepper
- 3 tbsps soy sauce
- dash of sugar
- 4 tbsps cooking oil

Instructions:

1. Mix first four ingredients and bring to boil until chicken feet are tender, adding water slowly as necessary (1/4 cup each time).

2. Sautee the remaining garlic in oil until light brown. Scoop the chicken feet and add to the pan and stir until tender, then add the sauce and simmer in medium heat for about 5 minutes adding soy sauce midway and the sugar close to the end.

  # dry chicken adobo

Prep Time: 20 minutes

Cooking Time: 45 minutes

Serves: 4 to 5

Ingredients:

- 1 head garlic, minced, separated
- 1kg whole chicken, cut into serving pieces
- 1/2 cup white vinegar
- 1/4 cup soy sauce
- 1 tsp black pepper corns
- 4 tbsps cooking oil
- 1 tbsp sugar
- salt to taste
- 2 hard-boiled eggs

Inang calls this "adobong tuyo." Not to be mistaken for the fish "tuyo," her term here refers to its literal meaning which is "dry." This is so because, there is very little adobo sauce in the dish when it is done.

Instructions:

1. Mix 6 cloves of minced garlic, vinegar, freshly ground black pepper and chicken in a casserole and let boil. Lower the heat and simmer for about 20 minutes or until the chicken pieces are cooked through.

2. Separate chicken from the sauce. Set aside.

3. Fry remaining garlic in cooking oil until golden brown. Set aside. Using the same pan, fry chicken pieces while stirring and until light brown in color. Lower the heat as necessary.

4. Add the separated adobo sauce. You may prefer to remove the spices from the sauce by straining them or simply spooning them away. Add, sugar and salt and cook for another 3-5 minutes. Top with hard-boiled eggs.

bistek tagalog

Prep Time: **15 minutes**	Cooking Time: **30 minutes**	Serves: **5 to 7**

Ingredients:

- 1kg beef tenderloin, cut in thin slices
- 2 large onions, sliced in rings (separated)
- 2 tbsps minced garlic
- 1/2 cup cooking oil

Marinate mixture:

- juice from 12–15 calamansi
- 1/2 cup soy sauce
- 1 tbsp sugar
- 1/2 tsp ground black pepper
- 1 tsp minced garlic

Instructions:

1. Marinate beef with mixture for half an hour.

2. Fry garlic slowly in cooking oil, add half the amount of sliced onions and cook until transparent.

3. Spoon beef slices from its maridate, add to pan and cook stirring until the juices of the meat come out.

4. Add the marinate and simmer until sauce thickens a bit. Top with remaining onions.

chicken afritada

Prep Time:
30 minutes

Cooking Time:
45 minutes

Serves:
3 to 4

Ingredients:

- 1kg chicken, cut into serving pieces
- 4 cloves garlic, minced
- 1 medium onion, diced finely
- 1 small tomato, deseeded and chopped finely
- 1 small carrot, cut diagonally
- 1 medium potato, quartered
- 1 small green bell pepper, diced roughly
- 1 small red bell pepper, diced roughly
- salt and ground pepper to taste
- 1 tbsp white vinegar
- 1 tsp soy sauce
- 1 tsp patis (optional)

Instructions:

1. Sautee garlic and onions until transparent. Add tomato and cook stirring until limp.

2. Add chicken pieces and soy sauce. Stir for about 10 minutes or until the juice drains from the chicken creating a little amount of sauce.

3. Add vinegar. Do not stir until it boils. Then add the vegetables. Stir once more.

4. Lower the heat and let simmer for about half an hour or until the chicken is cooked through and the vegetables tender.

Inang's tips:

Do not stir *after adding the vinegar. Only after it boils.*

The tomatoes should be seeded, otherwise it would produce water that would tamper the taste of the dish.

Use water very conservatively; it may not be necessary at all.

Let the chicken perspire, i.e., drain of its own juice.

 # tinolang manok

Prep Time:
20 minutes

Cooking Time:
35 minutes

Serves:
3 to 5

Ingredients:

- 1kg whole chicken, cut up
- 4 cloves garlic, minced
- 1 medium onion, diced finely
- 2-inch ginger, julienned
- 2 tbsps cooking oil
- salt and pepper
- patis
- 2 cups green papaya, cut into 3-inch slices
- fresh chili leaves
- 3 cups water

Replacements/Additions:

Papaya can be replaced with sayote.

Cubed potatoes can also be added to this dish.

Green chili leaves can be replaced with one serrano chili or malunggay leaves.

The amount of ginger can be reduced depending on your preference.

Patis has a magical effect on the over-all taste.

Instructions:

1. Over high heat, sautee ginger in cooking oil till light brown. Add garlic, stir for half a minute then add onions and cook stirring till transparent.

2. Add chicken pieces and cook till a bit browned. Add water, salt and pepper. Lower the heat, and simmer till the chicken is tender adding papaya and patis halfway and the chili leaves during the last 2 minutes of cooking.

menudo

Prep Time: 20 minutes

Cooking Time: 1.5 hours

Serves: 4 to 5

Ingredients:

- 1/2kg beef, diced
- 1/4kg beef liver, diced
- 1-2 pcs chicken liver, boiled and mashed
- 1/2 cup, chopped onions
- 4 garlic cloves, minced
- 1/2 cup chopped ripe tomatoes
- 1 cup diced potatoes
- 1/2 cup diced carrots
- salt to taste
- water
- 50g tomato paste
- 4 tbsps cooking oil
- 1/4 cup raisins
- 1/4 cup cooked green peas
  1/4 cup cooked chick peas (optional)
- bay leaf

Instructions:

1. Sautee garlic and onions in cooking oil till limp. Add tomatoes and cook stirring till it creates sauce, about 5 minutes.

2. Add beef and cook till tender, adding water as necessary.

3. Add beef liver, potatoes, carrots, bay leaf and salt. Stir. Add chicken liver, tomato paste and green peas.

beef asado

Prep Time: 40 minutes

Cooking Time: 4 hours

Serves: 5 to 7

Ingredients:

- 1kg chunk of beef
- 4 cloves garlic, minced
- 1 cup tomatoes, seeded and chopped
- 1 cup onion, minced
- juice of 4 calamansi or 1 lemon
- 1 tsp sugar
- 1/2 cup soy sauce
- 2 potatoes, peeled
- 2 small whole onions
- 2 tbsp pickle relish
- 25g tomato sauce
- 3 cups water

Instructions:

1. Marinate beef with minced onions, calamansi juice, soy sauce, sugar and tomatoes for at least an hour.

2. Sautee garlic till golden, add beef, turn once; add the marinate mixture, whole onions, potatoes and water and simmer under low fire till beef is about 75% done.

3. Add pickles and tomato sauce, then simmer again till sauce is thick and beef is tender. Let cool.

4. Slice beef. Pour sauce on top and garnish with fresh sliced onions and cooked potatoes.

bopis

Prep Time: 45 minutes

Cooking Time: 1 - 1 ½ minutes

Serves: 4 to 6

Ingredients:

- 1kg lungs of beef
- 1/4kg beef ears
- 1/4kg beef heart
- 8 cloves garlic, minced
- 2 medium onions, diced finely
- 1 medium tomato, diced finely
- 1 cup diced potatoes
- 1 cup diced carrot
- 1/2 cup diced red bell pepper
- vinegar to taste
- salt to taste
- freshly ground black pepper to taste
- 1 laurel leaf
- 1/4 cup achuete water
- 1/4 cup cooking oil

Instructions:

1. Boil beef lungs, heart and ears then cut them into small cubes, almost the size of the diced vegetables.

2. Sautee garlic and onions and stir for about two minutes. Add beef lungs, heart and ears, salt, black pepper and vinegar. Leave to boil then add the annatto water and laurel leaf. Lower the heat.

3. Simmer while stirring occasionally till meat are tender, adding tomatoes, potatoes and carrots halfway through, then the bell pepper when the first set of vegetables are half-done.

Inang replaces potatoes with white raddish. Makes the dish authentically different.

beef sinigang

Prep Time:
15 minutes

Cooking Time:
2-3 hours

Serves:
3 to 4

Ingredients:

- 1-1/2kg beef chunks, bone-in
- 2 medium onion, quartered
- 1 medium tomato, quartered
- a handful of fresh tamarind
- salt to taste
- 100g green or string beans, cut into 3-inch pieces
- 1 medium raddish, sliced thinly
- 1 medium eggplant, sliced
- 1 bunch kangkong or romaine lettuce
- 2-3 serrano chilis
- 5 cups water

Instructions:

1. Place onions, tomato, beef and water into a casserole and let boil. Lower the heat and continue to cook till meat are tender - about an hour and a half. Alternatively, use a pressure cooker.

2. Add the tamarind and salt, boil for another 10 minutes or until the tamarind starts to break apart. Do not overdo. Scoop the tamarind onto a bowl, add about a cup of water from the pot then mash. Strain the tamarind back onto the casserole/pot and discard the skin and seeds.

3. Add the string/green beans, chili, raddish and eggplant and simmer until vegetables are done.

4. Add patis (if using) and kangkong or romaine lettuce. Cook for half a minute and remove from fire.

This recipe is also good for chicken. One whole chicken cut up into 8 pieces would be best. The chicken (or beef) bones in the pot create a tastier soup.

morcon

Prep Time: 45 minutes

Cooking Time: 2 hours

Serves: 4 to 6

Ingredients:

- 1kg rib-eye steak, ¾ inch thick, about 8 inches in width
- 1 piece medium carrot, quartered into strips
- 4 pieces hotdogs (frankfurters), halved lengthwise
- 4 sweet pickled cucumber, halved lengthwise
- 4 salted eggs, quartered lenghtwise
- cheddar cheese, cut into 1/2-inch strips
- beef liver (optional), cut into 1/2-inch strips
- 1 tsp salt
- 1 tsp ground black pepper
- 1 tsp sugar
- juice from 2 lemons or 10 calamansi
- 1/2 cup soy sauce
- 1/2 cup cooking oil
- 8 cloves garlic, minced
- 4 medium onions, cut very finely
- 4 medium tomatoes, seeded and chopped (or one 14.5oz can chopped tomatoes)
- 1/4 cup tomato sauce

Instructions:

1. Mix lemon/calamansi juice, soy sauce, sugar, and pepper. Marinate beef steak in the mixture for at least two hours. Drain, but keep the liquid.

2. Place the steak on a flat surface or wide plate; line carrots, hotdogs, cheese, salted eggs, liver and cucumber next to each other on one end of the beef. Roll the beef and close the edges with cooking string. Make 4 rolls.

3. Using a deep casserole, sautee garlic and onion till the onion is transparent. Add tomatoes, stir for a couple of minutes and leave to cook for another 2 minutes or more. Add salt.

4. Arrange the morcon rolls with the mixture. Let boil then lower the heat. Add the marinating liquid to the pot. Simmer till beef is tender, adding water as necessary, but very sparingly. Add tomato sauce and simmer for 10 minutes turning beef occassionaly.

5. Let cool before cutting morcon. Pour sauce on top, or keep on the side.

kare-kare

Prep Time:
45 minutes

Cooking Time:
2 hours

Serves:
4 to 5

Ingredients:

- 1-1/2kg oxtail, beef tripe or beef cubes (or combination of any 2 or all)
- 1 fresh banana blossom, quartered and soaked in salted water for a few minutes and drained
- 1 bundle of pechay
- 2 cups string beans, cut into 3-inch pieces
- 4 medium eggplants, quartered
- 1 cup ground peanuts
- 1/2 cup peanut butter
- 4 cups water
- 1/2 cup annatto water
- 1/2 cup toasted ground rice (or toasted glutinous rice flour)
- 4 cloves garlic, minced
- 1-medium onion, quartered
- 1 medium onion, chopped
- 1/2 cup sauteed shrimp paste

Instructions:

1. Boil beef with quartered onions until meat becomes tender. Pressure cook is another option. Let cool a bit. Meanwhile, mix toasted ground rice, peanut butter and annatto water.

2. Sautee garlic and onions in a pan. Add beef pieces and stir once. Add half of the beef water, eggplants, banana blossom and string beans and simmer until half done.

3. Add the rice and peanut butter mixture and simmer until the sauce beomes thick.

4. Add pechay/bok choy. and cook until they are done.

5. Serve with shrimp paste on the side.

beef humba

Prep Time:
45 minutes

Cooking Time:
2 hours

Serves:
4 to 5

Ingredients:

- 1/4kg beef chunks, and 3/4kg cow's feet
- 1 large onion, diced roughly
- 6 cloves garlic, minced
- 1/4 cup soy sauce
- 1/2 cup vinegar
- 4 tbsps brown sugar
- 1/2 cup dried banana blossoms
- 2 pieces dried bay leaves (laurel leaves)
- 1 tbsp whole peppercorn
- 1 small bunch dried oregano
- 200g green beans (optional)
- 1 bunch of pechay leaves, blanched

Instructions:

1. Sautee garlic and onions in a saucepan and stir for about a minute.

2. Add beef chunks and feet and stir for a few more minutes.

3. Add the rest of the ingredients except banana blossoms and pechay. Lower the heat to medium and simmer till the meat are soft, about 3-4 hours. Alternatively, transfer them to a pressure cooker and cook till done—about 45 minutes.

4. Add dried banana blossoms, simmer for another 10 minutes.

5. Serve with steamed/blanched pechay.

Inang replaces beef chunks with oxtail in this recipe.

Cow's feet provide natural oil that makes the recipe tastier.

Some humba recipes call for salted black beans; Inang does not use them.

baka sa mais

Prep Time:
10 minutes

Cooking Time:
1 hr, 45 minutes

Serves:
3 to 5

Ingredients:

- 1kg cow's feet, cleaned
- 2 large (or 4 medium) onions, quartered
- 2 tbsp black peppercorns
- salt to taste
- 2-3 bunches leeks, cleaned
- 1-425g can sweet corn kernels (do not drain)
- 1-1/2 liters water

Instructions:

1. Bring water and onions to boil.

2. Add cow feet, lower heat and let simmer for 1.5 hours or till the meat is tender.

3. Add salt, peppercorns, leeks and corn kernels and continue to simmer for another 10 minutes.

beef tapa

Prep Time:
25 hours, including marinate time

Cooking Time:
15 minutes

Serves:
4 to 6

Ingredients:

- 1kg beef sirloin, sliced thinly
- 8 cloves garlic, minced
- 1/4 cup soy sauce
- 1/2 cup calamansi or lemon juice
- 2 tsp sugar
- salt and pepper
- 4 tbsp cooking oil

Instructions:

1. Mix soy sauce, calamansi/lemon juice, sugar, salt, pepper and garlic in a bowl and stir until sugar is dissolved. Add beef. Cover and refrigerate overnight, or for about 6 hours.

2. Heat cooking oil in a pan. Line beef slices on pan, leaving the marinate liquid aside. Fry both sides till slightly brown.

3. Beef tapa should be ready. At this point, you may want to add half the marinate liquid and continue to fry beef till all liquid evaporates. This process will make the beef tapa a bit sticky but tastier and less dry.

Parsley for a reason: *If you love the taste of garlic but dislike the smell it leaves in your mouth, you can chew a few leaves of parsley to get rid of the garlicky smell.*

Beef tapa is served with vinegar and minced garlic as dip and usually eaten with steamed rice.

It is also best with fried rice and sunny-side up egg on the side. Although usually a breakfast item, this dish is also good at any meal time.

beef with green bell pepper

Prep Time:
15 minutes

Cooking Time:
25 minutes

Serves:
4 to 6

Ingredients:

- 1/2kg beef sirloin, cut into 1-inch slices
- 2 tbsps minced garlic
- 1 medium onion, diced
- 1 cup green bell pepper, diced roughly
- salt and pepper to taste
- 2 tbsps oyster sauce
- 1/2 cup water

Instructions:

1. Sautee garlic and onion till transparent.

2. Add beef slices and cook, stirring till juices have almost evaporated. Add water and continue to cook if beef needs more time to become tender.

3. Add salt, pepper and oyster sauce and stir once.

4. Add bell pepper and water (if necessary at this point) and simmer for another couple of minutes or until the green peppers are half done.

fish and shellfish

pinangat na isda

Prep Time:
10 minutes

Cooking Time:
15 minutes

Serves:
3 to 4

Ingredients:

- 1/2kg fish, cleaned
- salt to taste
- 1/4 cup cooking oil
- 3 medium tomatoes
- 1/4 cup fresh tamarind juice
- fish sauce to taste (optional)

Instructions:

1. Halve one tomato. The other two remain whole.

2. Arrange all ingredients in a casserole and simmer till fish are done.

Tamarind juice can be replaced by fresh kamias.

Popular types of fish in Inang's kitchen for pinangat are ayungin (photos on the right and on next page) , sapsap, aligasin, talimu-sak dapa and mostly those without scales.

The same recipe is used for ayungin and other types of fish. Sapsap and ayungin, being small fishes, prove to be meticulous. But then, "good things are worth the trouble."

Pinangat na sapsap

Pinangat na ayungin

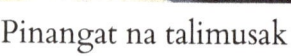

Pinangat na talimusak

Pinangat na dapa

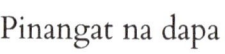

paksiw

Prep Time:
10 minutes

Cooking Time:
15 minutes

Serves:
4

Ingredients:

- 1kg fish, cleaned
- 2-inch ginger, pounded
- 1 tbsp salt
- 1/2 cup vinegar
- 2 pcs serrano chili

Instructions:

1. Arrange fish and chili in a casserole. Sprinkle with salt.

2. Add vinegar and ginger.

3. Simmer over medium heat till fish is done, about 10 minutes.

There are variations of this dish from different provinces in the Philippines. Some use garlic and/or onions, and a few add tomatoes. But paksiw's common ingredient is vinegar.

paksiw sa dilaw

Prep Time: 20 minutes

Cooking Time: 30 minutes

Serves: 4 to 6

Ingredients:

- 1kg eel
- salt to clean eel (about a cup)
- 6-8 cloves garlic, minced
- 1 medium onion, finely diced
- 2 tbsps fresh turmeric, grated
- 1 small tomato, chopped
- 1 cup white vinegar
- Salt and pepper to taste

Instructions:

1. Wash eel as you would any fish. Then cover skin with salt and rub until the slimy feel is gone. Wash in running water till salt is gone. Cut eel into 2-inch lengths.

2. Put eel, vinegar, salt and black pepper in a pot and let boil, then lower the heat. Simmer between 5-10 minutes depending on preferred doneness.

3. In another pot, sautee turmeric, garlic, onion and tomatoes (in that order) for a minute or two. Add eel mixture and simmer for 10-15 minutes.

Turmeric powder can be used instead of fresh turmeric. In this case, you would sautee garlic and onion, add turmeric powder, followed by tomatoes on step 3.

Adding water to this dish while cooking will result in watery or "syrupy" consistency. As you wish. :)

ginataang biya

 Prep Time:
15 minutes

 Cooking Time:
20 minutes

 Serves:
3 to 4

Ingredients:

- 1/2kg biya (goby)
- 3-inch size ginger, pounded
- salt to taste
- 1/2 cup white vinegar
- 1 cup coconut milk
- 2 pcs serrano chili

Instructions:

1. Arrange fish in a casserole. Sprinkle with salt, add ginger, and pour vinegar onto them. Simmer for about 4 minutes.

2. Add coconut milk and chili and simmer again for another 5 minutes or till the fish are cooked through.

3. Do not stir.

pesang dalag

Prep Time: **15 minutes**

Cooking Time: **20 minutes**

Serves: **3 to 5**

Ingredients:

- 1kg mud fish (dalag)
- 2-3 medium onions, quartered
- 2-inch ginger, sliced
- 1 big bunch of pechay (bok choy)
- 100g green beans (optional)
- 250g Chinese cabbage
- 1 tbsp whole black peppercorns
- 5-6 cups water
- salt to taste
- patis

Instructions:

1. Put onions, ginger, peppercorns in water and let boil.

2. Add fish and green beans. Lower the heat and simmer till fish is done – about 5 minutes.

3. Add the rest of the ingredients and simmer till vegetables are done.

Inang serves this with patis on the side to which I add sliced green chili. However, pesang dalag is mostly served with miso sauce on the side in some Pinoy households.

This dish is very much like tinolang manok (page 36) in its accompanying ingredients.
Mud fish is traditional for this dish, but any fish would do. I recommend the "meaty" fish types.

let's talk about sinigang

Sinigang is common in the Philippines. Every household must have prepared sinigang and every Filipino had tasted it. At times, I wonder why the Filipinos and the Philippines are associated with adobo rather than sinigang, with due respect to our adobo nation. But, yes, it should not matter. Wait, could it be because of the toyo (soy sauce)? If you are a non-Filipino, you may find it interesting to know what "toyo" connotes. Anyway, the term sinigang means "cooked in souring agent." The common souring agents in Filipino cooking are sampalok (tamarind), kamias (bilimbi), bayabas (guava), calamansi or lemon. Some use balimbing (star fruit) and/or santol (star apple).

Sinampalukan or binayabasan are common terms – they mean sinigang sa sampalok (tamarind) and sinigang sa bayabas (guava), respectively. To be more specific, "sinampalukang manok" means chicken sinigang in sampalok and "binayabasang bangus" simply means milkfish sinigang in guava.

Fish, shrimps, chicken and beef are all sinigang-friendly. Sampalok being the most used souring agent is good with all four meats - no fail. Having said that, fish is tastier with guava while beef is best with sampalok – not a limitation, but a preference. As for vegetables, you will notice that kangkong, chili, string or green beans are common to all sinigang no matter the souring agent. Radish, by the way is not as good with guava as it is than with sampaloc. Again, you may see this differently as it is simply a matter of taste. It is never a bad idea at all to experiment. Gabi (taro roots) are traditional, but can be optional. Eggplants is common in some provinces' sinigang mostly in the south.

So, sinigang and its variations have made the dish much more interesting.

sinigang sa sampalok

Prep Time:
15 minutes

Cooking Time:
25 minutes

Serves:
2 to 4

Ingredients:

- 1/2kg shrimps
- 1 medium tomato, quartered
- 1 medium onion, quartered
- a handful of fresh tamarind
- green or string beans cut to 3-inch pieces
- 1 medium raddish, sliced
- 1 medium eggplant, sliced
- 1 bunch kangkong
- 5 tbsp patis
- 2-3 serrano chilis
- 5 cups water

Instructions:

1. Put onion, tomato and tamarind in a casserole. Let boil until the tamarind are done – they will begin to break apart.

2. Scoop the tamarind in a bowl, add about a cup of soup water. Mash the tamarind. Strain the tamarind water onto the casserole/pot and discard the skin and seeds.

3. Add the string/green beans, chili, radish and eggplant and simmer till vegetables are done. Add the shrimps and cook for another 2-3 minutes.

4. Add patis and kangkong. Cook for half a minute and remove from fire.

  # sinigang sa bayabas

Prep Time:
15 minutes

Cooking Time:
25 minutes

Serves:
2 to 6

Ingredients:

- 1 bangus (milkfish) or other variety of fish (about 1kg)
- 1 medium tomato, quartered
- 1 medium onion, quartered
- 6-9 pcs over-ripe guavas
- green or string beans cut to 3" pieces and/or a few pieces of okra
- 1 bunch of kangkong
- 2 serrano chili
- 5 tbsp patis

Instructions:

1. Boil onion, tomato and guavas in a casserole or pot until the guavas start to tear.

2. Scoop the guavas in a bowl, add about a cup of soup water, then mash. Return to pot or strain, if you wish . I prefer straining them.

3. Add the milkfish, chili and string/green beans. Cook till fish is done; the beans would be good by then as well.

4. Add patis and kangkong. Cook for half a minute and remove from fire.

Inang puts back the mashed guavas to the pot to allow most of its taste in the soup. Then she scoops out the guava skin floating at the top and discards them.

 # bangus na may palaman

Prep Time:
45 minutes

Cooking Time:
30 minutes

Serves:
2 to 4

Ingredients:

- 1 medium bangus (milkfish)
- 1 medium onion, diced finely
- 1 medium tomato, diced finely
- 2 pcs serrano chili, cut finely
- salt to taste
- freshly ground black pepper, to taste
- cooking oil for sautéing and frying

Instructions:

1. Prepare the fish by trimming the tail, removing the gills and slicing from the top - head to tail - avoiding the stomach and spread it open and flat. Remove the entrails and clean in running water. Pat dry.

2. Mix the rest of the ingredients and spread onto the fish, making sure that you have enough to be able to fold the fish and the contents to not fall off.

3. Tie with kitchen string.

4. Gently fry the fish turning once when the first side is done.

This can be done in the grill; preferably wrapped in banana leaves.

Putting in the oven makes the vegetables water and the fish too wet. Indeed, thtat is why there is no oven in Inang's kitchen. :-)

escabeche

 **Prep Time:**
10 minutes

 **Cooking Time:**
15 minutes

Serves:
3 to 4

Ingredients:

- 1 whole fish (lapu-lapu, bangus, etc.), about 3/4kg, fried
- 1 medium onion, diced roughly
- 3 cloves garlic, minced
- 1-inch ginger, peeled and julienned
- salt and pepper to taste
- 1/2 cup pineapple juice
- 1/4 cup vinegar
- 1 tsp sugar
- 1 small red bell pepper, julienned
- 1 small green bell pepper, julienned
- 1/2 cup pineapple chunks

Instructions:

1. Mix pineapple juice, vinegar, sugar, salt and pepper in a bowl. Set aside.

2. Sautee ginger, garlic and onions (in that order) for half a minute each.

3. Add the bell peppers, stir for about a minute, add the sauce and the pineapple chunks. Let simmer for a few minutes.

4. Pour over fried fish.

Escabeche is best done with big types of fish lapu-lapu (grouper).

bidbid fishballs

Prep Time:
20 minutes

Cooking Time:
20 minutes

Serves:
4 to 6

Ingredients:

- 1kg fresh bidbid fish
- 1 medium onion, diced very finely
- 1 egg
- Salt and freshly ground black pepper to taste
- all-purpose flour for dusting

Instructions:

1. Scrape the meat from the fish and mash lightly.

2. Mix all ingredients, except the flour and form balls using hands. Flatten the balls, if you wish.

3. Roll in flour and fry in cooking oil.

4. Serve with your favorite dip. Catsup or sweet & sour dip are popular.

These fishballs can also be used for other dishes as escabeche, miswa soup, etc.

paez na bangus

Prep Time: 40 minutes

Cooking Time: 1 hour + 15 minutes

Serves: 8 to 12

Ingredients:

- 4 medium milkfish, (cleaned and deboned)
- 12 medium onions, diced finely
- 12 medium tomatoes, diced finely
- hot chili pepper, sliced/diced finely (to taste)
- salt and black pepper to taste
- 4 cups vinegar
- 40-45 whole young leaves of alagaw
- about 35 more alagaw leaves, cut finely

For the sauce:

- 5 tbsps flour
- 2 tbsps soy sauce
- 1/4 cup vinegar
- 1/4 cup water
- black pepper and sugar to taste

Instructions:

1. Mix onions, tomatoes, chili, salt, black pepper and cut alagaw leaves pressing them with your hands as you mix.

2. Place about 3 whole alagaw leaves in frying pan, then about 1 cup of the mix spreading them over the whole leaves. Place 2 bangus on top. Spread mix onto bangus enough to cover the fish, then cover with 2-3 whole leaves.

3. Place two remaining bangus on top of the whole leaves and repeat the process with 2-3 wholes leaves on top last.

4. Cover the pan and steam under medium heat for 1 hour.

5. Mix all the sauce ingredients thoroughly and cook over medium fire while stirring until the mix becomes thick in consistency.

paez na page, anyone?

Inang's original recipe for paez uses page (stingray). However, as the recipe is good and stingrays are not readily available, Inang tried the popular milkfish and it turned out to be similarly good.

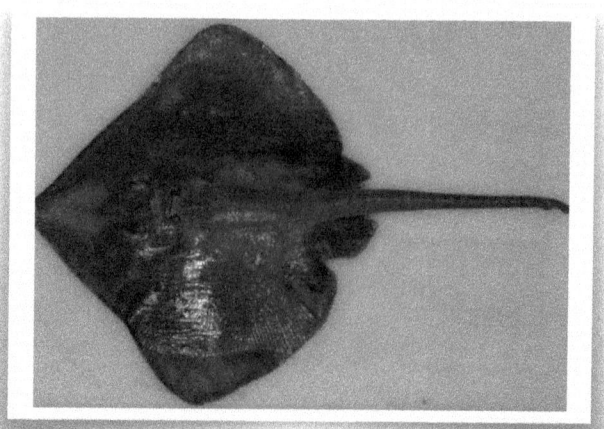

The only difference between cooking stingray and milkfish in this recipe is the way Inang cleans the stingray. The rest of the steps are the same.

The usual practice is that big stingrays are skinned before washing with water. However, Inang does it differently: she puts ash all over the stingray's skin and leaves it for a few minutes. This helps her in handling the stingray's slimy skin apart from ridding the stingray of its fishy smell. As if that is not enough, she showers the poor fish with vinegar (here we go again with the popular vinegar),

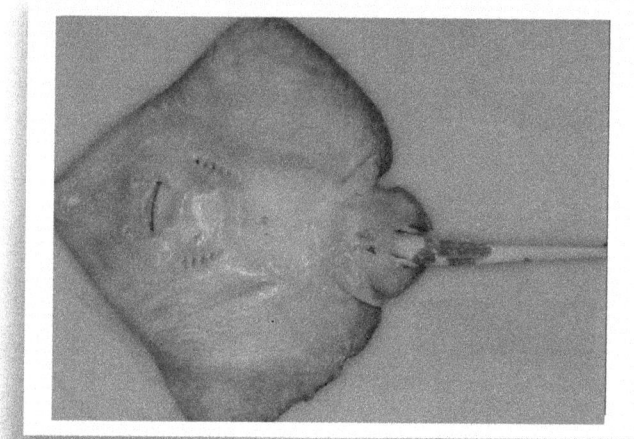

after skinning it and she washes it with water another time before cooking.

Yes, she cooks the whole stingray in paez. Unless dad takes home a really big one, then it is cut into about 5-ince pieces before being paez'ed!!

This is worth trying.

fish sarciado

Prep Time: 20 minutes

Cooking Time: 30 minutes

Serves: 4 to 5

Ingredients:

- 1kg fish, any type, fried
- 4 cloves garlic, minced
- 1 medium onion
- 1/4kg fresh ripe tomatoes, chopped
- 3 tbsps chopped parsley
- salt and pepper to taste
- 3 tbsp cooking oil
- 2 tbsp fish sauce

Instructions:

1. Saute garlic in oil for half a minute. Add onions and stir for 2 more minutes or until the onions become transparent.

2. Add tomatoes and cook till the mixture combines well. Add salt and pepper. Stir.

3. Remove from heat and add chopped parsley. Stir again.

4. Sprinkle cooked mixture over fried fish.

5. Best served with plain rice and fried eggplants on the side.

Magida used fish fillet in the photos above. Francis' sarciadong bikaw (type of fish) photo on next page.

luto sa toyo

Prep Time:
20 minutes

Cooking Time:
20 minutes

Serves:
2 to 3

Ingredients:

- 1 medium bangus (milkfish), about 1kg
- 1 large onion, diced finely
- 4 cloves garlic, minced
- freshly ground black pepper, to taste
- juice from 2 lemons or 12 calamansi
- 1/2 cup soy sauce
- 1/8 cup cooking oil
- fresh onion rings to garnish

Instructions:

1. Clean the fish, cut into 3 pieces, width-wise. Dry with towel paper, sprinkle with salt (to taste) and fry till golden brown. Keep aside.

2. Sautee garlic and onion in cooking oil till a bit golden – 4-5 minutes.

3. Add lemon/calamansi juice, soy sauce, black pepper and simmer for a minute. Do not stir.

4. Pour over fried bangus.

tortang tulya

Prep Time: 45 minutes

Cooking Time: 20 minutes

Serves: 2 to 4

Ingredients:

- 1/2kg tulya (small clams)
- 1 large onion, diced finely
- 1 medium onion, quartered
- 5 cloves garlic, minced
- salt and pepper to taste
- 4 eggs
- 1/4 cup cooking oil (can be used sparingly)
- 1/2 cup water
- 100g butter or margarine

Instructions:

1. Clean the clams by letting them in running water for a few minutes. Then put them in a casserole with 1/2 cup water, butter (or margarine), and quartered onions. Let boil uncovered till the shells open up. Get the meat from the clams and ditch the shells; water can be used as soup later. Grind clam meat coarsely, or to your preference.

2. Sautee garlic and onion till onions are translucent. Mix clams, add salt and pepper.

3. Beat the eggs. Add salt and pepper.

4. Spread half the beaten eggs in a pan as if making crepes. Spread 1/2 of the clam mixture in the middle and fold the edges of the eggs towards the center. Repeat. Makes two tortang tulya.

The same recipe can be used for Tortang Hipon by using steamed shrimps instead of clams.

 # ginataang alimasag

Prep Time:
15 minutes

Cooking Time:
20 minutes

Serves:
3 to 4

Ingredients:

- 1kg alimasag (crabs), about 6 crabs, halved
- 1 medium onion, diced finely
- 3 cloves garlic, minced
- salt to taste
- 4 tbsps patis
- 1 cup coconut milk
- 200g butternut squash
- 1 bunch of kangkong leaves (water spinach)
- 100g string beans
- 2 pcs serrano chili
- 1/2 cup coconut cream
- 3 tbsps cup cooking oil

Instructions:

1. Sautee garlic and onions in cooking oil. Add string beans, squash and coconut milk. Let boil over medium heat.

2. Add crabs and continue to simmer till done, about 6 minutes.

3. Add coconut cream simmer for about three minutes, then add the kangkong leaves, chili, salt, pepper and patis. Simmer again for another minute.

tortang alimasag

Prep Time: **45 minutes**

Cooking Time: **30 minutes**

Serves: **8**

Ingredients:

- meat from steamed alimasag (crabs)– about 8 crabs (keep the shells)
- 1 large onion, diced very finely
- 1 medium carrot, diced finely
- 1 medium potato, diced finely
- 5 cloves garlic, minced
- salt and pepper to taste
- 2 eggs, beaten (divided)
- 1/2 cup cooking oil (divided)
- 1/4 cup water

Instructions:

1. Pre-boil carrots and potatoes then drain.

2. Sautee crab meat with garlic and onion. Add salt and pepper. Let cool, then mix with one beaten egg, pre-boiled carrots and potatoes.

3. Fill crab shells with mixture and brush with beaten egg.

4. Fry top side down in remaining cooking oil.

alimango sa miswa

Prep Time:
10 minutes

Cooking Time:
15 minutes

Serves:
2 to 4

Ingredients:

- 1kg alimango (crabs), halved or opened
- 4 cloves garlic, minced
- 1 medium onion, diced
- salt and pepper to taste
- 2 cups water
- 200g miswa noodles
- patis

Instructions:

1. Sautee garlic and onions for about 2 minutes.

2. Add fresh alimango and stir once.

3. Add water and simmer till the crabs are half done.

4. Add miswa and continue to simmer for another minute.

5. Add salt, pepper and patis.

adobong pusit

 **Prep Time:** 15 minutes

 **Cooking Time:** 20 minutes

 **Serves:** 3 to 5

Ingredients:

- 1kg pusit (squid), cleaned
- 1/2 cup vinegar
- 1/4 cup soy sauce
- 6 cloves garlic, minced
- 1 small onion, sliced or diced roughly
- 1 small tomato, diced
- salt and pepper to taste
- 1 tsp sugar
- 2-3 tbsps cooking oil

Instructions:

1. Sautee garlic in vegetable oil till golden. Add onions and cook until they are transparent, followed by tomatoes. Add squid, turn once, then add vinegar and soy sauce. Do not stir until after it boils.

2. Add salt, pepper and sugar.

a fishy story

My brother-in-law, Mike, while in the US in the mid 80's, took his girlfriend to a Filipino restaurant at her request. Determined to show her the authenticity of Filipino food, he ordered a variety of dishes including fish sinigang. With excitement at both the food and his audience, Mike proceeded to fondle the fish, removing the bones and giving her pieces of fish meat to sample. All was going well until he picked up the head of the lapu-lapu (grouper) sinigang and started to suck the eye of the fish. Mike later came out of the restaurant, not having finished his dinner, without a girlfriend!

Eating fish could be a skill second only to its preparation. Removing the scales, deboning it during meal - you name it - they can be truly intricate. It all starts at the market where one must know how to identify the fresh from the stale? It makes a hell of a difference.

Most people think the supermarket is not the place for "fresh" fish except maybe for live tilapia; but tilapia is as common as our national fish, bangus (milk fish), which is dead almost immediately after being caught. However, bangus won't go stale even if exposed the whole day as compared to mudfish that should be cleaned alive; it's not good for consumption if the poor fish is dead before buying. "Bangus is safe," says my father who grew up in the "palaisdaan" and "pamamalakaya." I guess his roots explain my inherent love for seafood.

The fish market, on the other hand, is always exciting with its variety of fish. Preparing the fish, cooking and getting the right taste are always gratifying challenges. I do not overdo the ingredients for each fish recipe because I do not want the ingredients to take over its natural taste. The ingredients and cooking should enhance the fish rather than cover its fishy-ness.

We all know, the place where and how the seafood is caught affects the price. Where a fish is caught also makes a difference in taste. Pinangat na ayungin, small fish from Laguna Lake - this variety is smaller than the ayunging dagat that has green stripes. The former's meat is more tender. The fresh water fish is normally more tender than the salt water fish - somehow the norm, but that does not necessarily make it better than the other. Similarly, for shrimps caught from the sea against cultured shrimps.

There is a quickly growing demand for fish fillet meals being served by food stands to fast-food outlets to your favorite restaurants. However, the fish fillet wasn't initially locally produced. It is fleshy, boneless, bland but convenient and easy, both for the eating public and those who serve it. There isn't much praises for this fish even on the Internet. You and I would always be better off devouring a whole fresh fish that we pick up that day in the market.

Be adventurous, step in the wet market and find the joy in picking up the fish with the best looking set of eyes.

by Francis Perez

pastas and noodles

pastas and noodles

 # *pancit sa achuete*

Prep Time: 15 minutes

Cooking Time: 20 minutes

Serves: 3 to 5

Ingredients:

- 1/2kg pancit bihon, (rice noodles) soaked in water then drained
- 1/4kg boneless chicken, cut into 1/2-inch pieces
- 3 cloves garlic, minced
- 1 medium onion, cut finely
- salt and pepper to taste
- achuete (annatto seed water)
- 3 tbsps. cooking oil
- 2 tbsps. patis
- 2 tbsps. parsley leaves, cut finely

Instructions:

1. Saute garlic and onions in cooking oil over medium heat for about 2 minutes. Add chicken pieces and stir until the juices in the chicken are drained. Add salt and pepper followed by achuete water and mix thoroughly.

2. Add noodles immediately; stirring constantly until the achuete colors the noodles. Stir for further 3 minutes or until the noodles are cooked.

3. Add patis (be careful not to make the dish salty).

4. Sprinkle with parsley leaves before serving.

Achuete, or annatto seeds, are soaked in warm water for a few minutes to extract the light red or orange color.

lomi

Prep Time: 15 minutes

Cooking Time: 20 minutes

Serves: 4 to 5

Ingredients:

- 1/4kg lomi noodles (miki), washed in running water and drained
- 4 cloves garlic, minced
- 2 portions chicken breasts, cut into 1/2-inch strips
- 1/4 cup chicken liver, sliced thinly
- 1 medium onion, cut into slices
- 1 small red bell pepper, diced
- 1 small green bell pepper, diced
- 1 medium carrot, julienned
- 1/4 cup green beans, cut diagonally
- 1/2 cup cabbage, cut roughly
- 1/4 cup corn flour, mixed with 3 tbsp water
- 1 egg, beaten
- salt and pepper to taste
- 4 tbsp patis
- 2 hard-boiled eggs, sliced, for garnish

Instructions:

1. Sautee garlic and onions for 2 minutes. Add chicken and stir again until the meat is opaque in color. Add chicken liver and cook stirring constantly till done.

2. Add carrots and green beans and cook for about 2 minutes. Add bell peppers and cabbage, and noodles stir and cook for another 2 minutes.

3. Add salt, black pepper and patis and stir once. Add corn flour and stir another time, followed by beaten egg and stir again.

4. Top with hard-boiled eggs. (Option: Crack one egg onto the cooked dish and let cook from its heat.

pancit gisado

Prep Time: 30 minutes

Cooking Time: 30 minutes

Serves: 6 to 8

Ingredients:

- 225g bihon noodles, soaked in water
- 150g canton noodles
- 6 garlic cloves, minced
- 1 medium sized onion, sliced
- 3/4kg boneless chicken, cut into small pieces
- 1 cup chicken broth
- 1 cup carrots, julienned
- 1 cup green beans, julienned
- 1 cup cauliflower, cut into florets
- 1/2 cup snow peas (optional)
- 1/2 cup dried mushrooms (black fungus type), soaked in water
- 1/2 cup fresh parsley to garnish
- 1/4 cup patis
- 1/4 cup soy sauce
- 1/4 cup oyster sauce
- salt and pepper, to taste
- calamansi

Instructions:

1. Sautee garlic and onions for about 2 minutes.

2. Add chicken, stir until the juices come out. Add soy sauce, vegetables (except cabbage), salt and pepper and stir until the vegetables are just about half-done.

3. Add oyster sauce, stir once, then add broth, patis and bihon noodles. Stir until completely mixed and the noodles just done. Add canton noodles and cabbage and stir until all are cooked through.

4. Transfer to serving plate and serve with calamansi on the side.

Another option is to pre-boil chicken (bone in) and one bulb of young onion with 2-3 cups of water. Debone the chicken. Use the meat and broth accordingly.

 # corned beef macaroni

Prep Time:
10 minutes

Cooking Time:
10 minutes

Serves:
3 to 5

Ingredients:

- 2 cans 210g corned beef
- 300g elbow macaroni, boiled and drained
- 4 cloves garlic, minced
- 1 large white onion, divided (dice half the onion and slice the other half)
- 3 tbsp cooking oil
- salt and pepper to taste

Instructions:

1. Sautee garlic in cooking oil for half a minute followed by onion and stir till transparent.

2. Add corned beef and cook stirring for about a couple of minutes.

3. Add macaroni, salt and pepper. Stir again and add sliced onions during the last minute of cooking.

 # pancit luglug

Prep Time:
30 minutes

Cooking Time:
45 minutes

Serves:
4 to 5

Ingredients:

- 1kg sotanghon or bihon noodles
- 1/4 kg ground beef
- 2 cups shrimp juice
- 4 cloves garlic, minced
- 1 medium onion, diced finely
- salt and pepper to taste
- 2 cups glutinous rice flour
- 1/2 cup annatto water, divided
- 1 cup water
- 1/2 cup cooking oil
- 1/2 cup calamansi juice mixed with 1/4 cup patis

● Toppings:

- 1 cup chicharon, crushed
- 1/4kg shrimps, steamed, peeled and halved
- 3 hard-boiled eggs, sliced
- 1/2 cup spring onions, chopped finely
- 2 tbsp fried garlic
- calamansi slices

Instructions:

1. Prepare noodles according to package instructions, i.e., sotanghon is soaked in water for a few minutes while bihon is blanched lightly. Sprinkle with calamansi/patis mixture and set aside.

2. Sautee garlic and onion. Add shrimp juice and simmer until the sauce curdles. Add ground beef and cook for a few more minutes followed by annatto water, salt and pepper.
Continue to simmer and set aside.

3. Mix glutinous rice flour with one cup water. The mixture should be runny, so feel free to add water as necessary. Cook stirring until the mixture becomes a bit thick but not heavy. Set aside.

4. Serve by portioning each plate with enough noodles. Top with rice flour sauce, ground beef mixture, spring onions, shrimps, boiled eggs and fried garlic and calamansi on the side.

pancit malabon

Prep Time: 45 minutes

Cooking Time: 40 minutes

Serves: 4 to 5

Ingredients:

* 1kg thick rice noodles
* 1/4kg ground beef
* 3 cups shrimp water
* 6 cloves garlic, minced
* 1 large onion, diced finely
* salt and pepper to taste
* 1/4 cup annatto water
* 1/2 cup cooking oil
* 1/2 cup calamansi juice mixed with 1/4 cup patis
* 2 cups Chinese cabbage, shredded lightly
*

Toppings:

* 1 cup chicharon, crushed
* 1/2kg shrimps, steamed, peeled and halved
* 1/2 kg squid, cooked (adobo would be best)
* 6 hard-boiled eggs, sliced
* 1/2 cup spring onions, chopped finely
* 4 tbsps fried garlic
* calamansi slices

Instructions:

1. Ready noodles according to package instructions.

2. Sautee garlic and onion in cooking oil. Add shrimp water and let boil till they curdle.

3. Add ground beef and cook for a few more minutes. Add annatto water, salt and pepper and simmer. Scoop out beef and curdled shrimp juice and set aside, leaving the oil in the pan.

4. Mix the noodles with oil in pan. Add half the amount of the Chinese cabbage and calamansi juice/patis mixture. Stir to coat noodles with the mixture. Put back the cooked ground beef/shrimp juice and mix.

5. Place in a serving plate big enough to accommodate the noodles and cover with its toppings arranging them nicely

6. Design with remaining Chinese cabbage and the rest of the toppings.

7. Serve with calamansi on the side.

vegetables

ginisang ampalaya

Prep Time: 20 minutes

Cooking Time: 20 minutes

Serves: 3 to 5

Ingredients:

- 2 medium ampalaya (bitter gourd) - about 300g
- 3 cloves garlic, minced
- 1 medium onions, diced finely
- 1 small tomato, seeded and chopped
- salt to taste
- 1/4 tbsp ground black pepper
- 2 eggs
- 1/4 cup water
- 4 tbsps cooking oil
- 4 tbsp patis

Instructions:

1. Cut ampalaya lengthwise, remove the seeds then slice diagonally and soak in salted water for a few minutes. The longer you soak, the less of the natural bitter taste of the ampalaya will remain). Drain in a colander.

2. Sautee garlic, onions and tomatoes, one minute in between.

3. Add eggs and stir while breaking them into smaller pieces.

4. Add ampalaya, salt, pepper, water and patis. Stir lightly.

A few ways to remove the bitter taste of ampalaya are pre-soaking them in salted water, washing them off and cooking them longer after step 4.

Ampalaya are deep green in color when half-done while they become slightly yellow when cooked further. Half-cooked ampalaya would be bitter by comparison.

 # kilawing labanos

Prep Time:
15 minutes

Cooking Time:
20 minutes

Serves:
3 to 5

Ingredients:

- 1 small onion, chopped
- 1kg labanos (raddish), julienned
- 1/2kg fresh shrimps, shelled, deveined and sliced
- shrimp water from shrimp heads, but using 1/2 cup vinegar instead (see page 92)
- 3 cloves garlic, minced
- 1 medium-sized onion,
- diced finely
- salt and pepper to taste
- 1/2 cup annatto water
- patis

Instructions:

1. Mix annatto water and labanos in a bowl to result in an orange color for the labanos.

2. Sautee garlic and onions. Add shrimp/ vinegar extract. Do not stir until the mixture curdles, then add shrimps. Cook till shrimps are pinkish in color.

3. Add labanos and the rest of the ingredients. Lower the heat and simmer for 10-12 minutes, or till the labanos are done.

The color of the dish is dependent on the use of achuete water and vinegar.

ginisang bitsuwelas

Prep Time: 20 minutes

Cooking Time: 25 minutes

Serves: 4 to 5

Ingredients:

- 1/2kg bitsuwelas (greenbeans)
- 1/4kg small shrimps , or 1/2 cup shrimp water
- 1 medium onion, diced finely
- 3 cloves garlic, minced
- 1 small tomato, seeded and diced
- salt and pepper to taste
- 1 tbsp patis
- 3 tbsp cooking oil

Instructions:

1. Extract shrimp water (if using) by following instructions on page 92.

2. Sautee garlic and onion and stir for about 2 minutes. Add shrimps or shrimp juice. Do not stir until the mixture curdles, if using shrimp water.

3. Add diced tomato and bitsuwelas, stir occasionally and cook till bitsuelas are tender.

4. Add salt, pepper and patis.

This is Inang's basic ginisa recipe for most vegetables.

Other vegetables good for this recipe are gourd, string beans, chayote, papaya, cabbage, green/ red bell pepper, carrots, cauliflower or any combination of two or more vegetables mentioned.

 # cauliflower with sotanghon

Prep Time: 15 minutes

Cooking Time: 20 minutes

Serves: 3 to 4

Ingredients:

- 100g sotanghon noodles soaked in water
- 1 head cauliflower, cut into florets
- 4 cloves garlic, minced
- 1 medium sized onion, diced finely
- 1 small tomato, deseeded and chopped
- 1/4kg shrimps, shelled and deveined
- salt and black pepper to taste
- 2 tbsps patis
- 1/2 cup achuete water

Instructions:

1. Sautee garlic, onions and tomato for about 2 minutes. Add shrimps and stir till pinkish in color.

2. Add cauliflower stirring for a few seconds, then add achuete water, salt, pepper and patis. Let simmer until the the cauliflower are cooked to your preferred doneness.

ginataang puso ng saging
(Banana blossoms in coconut milk)

Prep Time: 20 minutes **Cooking Time:** 30 minutes **Serves:** 4 to 6

Ingredients:

- 2 medium banana blossoms
- 1/4kg shrimps, shelled, deveined and sliced or diced
- 1 medium onions, diced finely
- 4 cloves garlic, minced
- coconut milk from 2 coconuts or 150-oz can coconut milk
- 3 tbsps cooking oil
- 3/4 cup vinegar
- salt and pepper to taste
- 2 tbsps fish sauce
- Serrano chili (optional)

Instructions:

1. Halve the banana blossoms lengthwise, then cut cross-wise, about 1/2 inch in size. Put them in salted water for a few minutes. Drain.

2. Saute garlic and onions in cooking oil. Stir for about two minutes, then add shrimps and continue to stir until the shrimps are pinkish in color.

3. Add vinegar, lower the heat and let boil for only a very few seconds. Do not stir.

4. Add the banana blossoms and chili, if using. Simmer for a couple of minutes then add the coconut milk; simmer again until cooked through ading salt, pepper and patis in between.

Water can be added to the dish, if preferred. This would lightly tame the vinegar taste.

pinakbet

Prep Time:
15 minutes

Cooking Time:
20 minutes

Serves:
3 to 4

Ingredients:

- 4 cloves garlic, minced
- 1 medium onion, sliced
- 1 medium tomato, chopped
- 1 medium ampalaya, sliced
- 1-1/2 cup, string beans or green beans, cut into 3-inch pieces
- 1 cup pumpkin, cut up to 1-inch pieces
- 1-2 eggplants, cut into 2-inch slices
- 1 cup okra, cleaned
- 2 tbsps fresh bagoong
- 1/4kg fresh shrimps
- salt and/or patis to taste

- 1-2 cups water

Instructions:

1. Sautee garlic, onions and bagoong and cook for two minutes stirring. Add tomatoes and shrimps.

2. Add vegetables giving allowance to the ones that cook first. Stir once and add water. Cook until all vegetables are done to your preference.

3. Add salt and/or patis and adjust the taste.

The vegetables can be a bit done or overdone, as you prefer, the taste continues to be good.

adobong kangkong

Prep Time:
15 minutes

Cooking Time:
20 minutes

Serves:
3 to 4

Ingredients:

- 1 bunch of kangkong, about 250g
- 4 cloves garlic, minced
- 1/4 cup white vinegar
- 3 tbsps soy sauce
- 1/2 tsp sugar
- 3 tbsps cooking oil
- ground black pepper
- fried garlic to garnish

Instructions:

1. Sautee garlic in cooking oil until brown.

2. Add vinegar, soy sauce, sugar and black pepper. Let boil without stirring.

3. Add kangkong stalks and cook for about two minutes, then add kangkong leaves. Let simmer for another half a minute.

4. Transfer to a plate and garnish with fried garlic.

The kangkong can be half done or overdone when cooking with both the leaves and stems.

An interesting option is cooking only the stems in adobo and use the leaves for another recipe.

The crunchy garlic garnish creates a teasing contrast in the mouth.

substitute for shrimps

Some or the recipes in this book call for either shrimp or shrimp water (also called shrimp juice). Shrimp is usually the first choice while its juice a substitute. Exceptions are pancit luglug (page 79) and pancit malabon (page 81) where the recipes ask for both the shrimps and shrimp water.

Shrimps are expensive, relatively. So the shrimp water was born. You might wonder, "shrimp water is from shrimps!" We understand that. Imagine the savings in this idea: when we use shrimps in a recipe, we put the shrimp heads aside to create shrimp water for another recipe.

One good practice is to use "uluhan" as they produce more shrimp juice! Uluhan (photo below) are less than an inch in size, their heads and eyes bigger than usual, the rostrum more pointed and the carapace (shell of the head) hard. They are also cheaper than the regular shrimps. We use uluhan straight to create the shrimp water.

Below are instructions to make shrimp water or shrimp juice:

- Pound the shrimps using mortar and pestle (or use the blender or mini-chopper)

- Mix with water (or vinegar, as the recipe calls for)

- Squeeze and drain to get the juice.

ginisang munggo

Prep Time:
10 minutes

Cooking Time:
20 minutes

Serves:
4

Ingredients:

- 2 cups pre-boiled munggo
- 3 tbsp cooking oil
- 3 cloves garlic, minced
- 1 medium-sized onion, diced finely
- 1 small tomato, diced
- 1/4kg, shrimps, peeled and deveined
- 1-2 cups water
- 4 tbsps patis
- salt and pepper to taste
- ampalaya leaves

Instructions:

1. Sautee garlic, onion and tomato -- in that order, with a distance of about half a minute each.

2. Add shrimps and stir till they are pinkish in color.

3. Add munggo, water, salt, pepper and patis and simmer. Add ampalaya leaves then turn off the heat immediately.

This recipe is also good for any variety of lentils.

Note: in the photo above, 3 thin slices of ampalaya are used to replace leaves and 3 paksoy leaves are added.

talbos ng kamote

Prep Time: 10 minutes

Cooking Time: 10 minutes

Serves: 1-2

Ingredients:

- 300g talbos ng kamote (sweet potato tops)
- 1/2 cup water
- 4 tbsps cooking oil
- 3 tbsps patis
- juice of 5-6 calamansi or 1 lemon

Instructions:

1. Clean and wash talbos and place in a casserole with water, cooking oil and patis.

2. Simmer till the talbos are done.

3. Add calamansi/lemon juice.

Talbos ng kamote are usually just steamed and served with fried fish. We also eat this by itself as an appetizer. Just can't wait!

sweets and snacks

tabayayong

Prep Time:
15 minutes

Cooking Time:
1.5 hours

Serves:
5

Ingredients:

- 2 cups pre-boiled munggo (mung beans)
- 1 cup grated fresh coconut (or desiccated coconut)
- 1-1/2 cups sugar
- 2 tbsps butter or margarine
- 2 tbsps vanilla (optional)

Instructions:

1. Mix coconut meat and sugar in a wide pan and stir till they are completely combined and the coconut is a bit cooked. The consistency would be kind of sticky.

2. Add mung beans and stir frequently until almost dry, around 10-15 minutes.

3. Add butter or margarine and continue to stir to desired consistency.

4. Spread on individual plates; flatten them with buttered spoon.

5. Can be served hot or cold.

The same recipe is used for Turong Munggo on the following page.

turong munggo

 **Prep Time:**
30 minutes

 **Cooking Time:**
20 minutes

 **Serves:**
8 to 10

Ingredients:

- servings of Tabayayong
  (recipe on preceding page)
- lumpia wrapper
  (spring roll pastry)

Instructions:

1. Roll about 2 tablespoons of mixture in a lumpia wrapper sealing the edges.

2. Deep fry in cooking oil.

3. Can be served hot or cold.

turong saging

Prep Time:
20 minutes

Cooking Time:
10 minutes

Serves:
8 to 12

Ingredients:

- 12 pieces saging na saba (plantains)
- 12 sheets spring roll pastry
- langka (jackfruit) pieces, sliced
- 1/2cup sugar
- 1 tsp flour in1/4 cup water for sealing edges of wrapper
- cooking oil for deep frying

Instructions:

1. Halve plantains lengthwise.

2. Place on top of a spring roll pastry sheet, top with langka slices and sprinkle with sugar. Wrap and seal the edges.

3. Deep fry till golden.

4. Serve warm, while the wrapper is still crispy and the plantain soft. It's a good tease to the mouth.

sumang kamoteng kahoy

Prep Time:
45 minutes

Cooking Time:
45 minutes

Serves:
8 to 12

Ingredients:

- 2 cups shredded cassava
- 1 cup grated coconut (or dessicated coconut)
- 2-1/2 cups sugar
- 1 cup coconut milk
- banana leaves for wrapping

Instructions:

1. Ready banana leaves by cleaning them and cutting them to about 3X4" squares.

2. Mix all ingredients in a bowl.

3. Scoop about 2 tbsps of mixture onto a piece of banana leaf and wrap by rolling and folding the edges over to close.

4. Steam between 30-45 minutes.

5. Can be served hot or cold.

For easier handling, banana leaves can be slightly heated on the stove before using to wrap suman mixture

champorado

Prep Time:
10 minutes

Cooking Time:
20 minutes

Serves:
2 to 3

Ingredients:

- 1 cup glutinous rice (malagkit)
- 2/3 cup sugar
- 2 tbsp cocoa powder, mixed with 1/4 cup water
- 3 cups water

Instructions:

1. Cook glutinous rice in water stirring frequently until done. The consistency should be runny, so do add water as necessary.

2. Add cocoa followed by sugar and stir consistently until they are thoroughly mixed.

3. Serve with fresh milk or evap milk.

Tablea or cooking chocolate can be used instead of cocoa powder.

Champorado is both a breakfast or a snack choice.

Champorado is also popularly served with fried tuyo (sun-dried sardine fish).

ginatang mais

Prep Time:
5 minutes

Cooking Time:
30 minutes

Serves:
4

Ingredients:

• 2 cups coconut milk
• 1 cup coconut cream
• 1 cup corn kernels
• 1/2 cup glutinous rice (malagkit)
• 1/2 cup water
• 2/3 cup sugar

Instructions:

1. Mix coconut milk, water and rice in a casserole/pot. Let boil then lower the heat. Stir every now and then until the rice is cooked. The consistency should be light, creamy soup-like.

2. Add sugar slowly and continue to stir. Then add corn kernels and coconut cream. Simmer for about 3 minutes.

Option: Use 1/2 cup corn kernels and 1/2 cup cream style corn.

ginatang halo-halo

Prep Time:
20 minutes

Cooking Time:
30 minutes

Serves:
3 to 5

Ingredients:

- 2 cups coconut milk
- 1-1/2 cups water
- 1/2 cups kamote (sweet potatoes), diced
- 1/2 cup diced gabi (taro roots) - optional
- 1 cup saba (cooking banana/plantain), sliced
- 1/2 cup langka (jackfruit), sliced
- 1/2 cup pre-cooked sago (tapioca pearls)
- 10-15 pieces bilo-bilo (glutinous rice balls)*
- 2/3 cup sugar

Instructions:

1. Boil water in a big casserole/pot. Lower the heat to medium and add half the amount of coconut milk and wait until it boils again.

2. Add kamote, gabi and bilo-bilo and cook for about five minutes.

3. Add the remaining coconut milk, stir once and add sugar slowly. Simmer for a couple of minutes.

4. Put-in the jack fruit and sago. Stir once and simmer for no more than a minute.

5. Serve hot.

(Pre-cooked) Sago are available in the local market.

Bilo-bilo are glutinous rice flour mixed with water and shaped into balls. They are also available in the local market pre-mixed. They also come in purple color or plain white.

 # ginatang munggo

Prep Time.
10 minutes

Cooking Time:
45 minutes

Serves:
3 to 4

Ingredients:

- 1/2 cup munggo (mung beans)
- 2 cups coconut milk
- 1/2 cup glutinous rice (malagkit)
- 1/2 cup water
- 1 cup sugar

Instructions:

1. Roast munggo in a pan till golden brown. Let cool.

2. Crack the roasted munggo using a mortar and pestle. Set aside.

3. Simmer coconut milk, water and glutinous rice in a pot until the rice is tender. Mix sugar and munggo and cook further stirring occasionally till the ingredients are very well mixed.

4. Serve hot.

biko

Prep Time:
10 minutes

Cooking Time:
30-45 minutes

Serves:
3 to 6

Ingredients:

- 2 cups glutinous rice, washed and drained
- 2 tbsps coconut oil
- 3 cups coconut milk
- 2 cups water
- 1-1/2 cups dark brown sugar
- dash of salt

Toppings:
- Latik* or grated fresh coconut

Instructions:

1. Mix rice, coconut milk, salt and water in a pan over medium heat. Stir and let boil. Continue stirring until rice is cooked but not dry.

2. Slowly add sugar and continue to stir until it reaches the consistency that you want. Inang's gauge is when the mixture turns quite rubbery – no more liquid, but not dry.

3. Move the biko onto a bigger dish, preferably covered with banana leaves to prevent from sticking. Flatten with the use of an oiled spoon. Let cool before cutting into portions. Top with latik or grated fresh coconut.

*Latik is achieved by slowly bringing 2 (or more) cups of coconut cream to boil and stirring it until oil and latik are formed. Scoop the latik away from the oil and use them as needed.